A PICTORIAL MEMOIR

OF

B.W. NEWTON

A PICTORIAL MEMOIR
OF
B.W. NEWTON

Supplement to

'A Guide to the Works and Remains of Benjamin Wills Newton'

Compiled by

C.W.H. Griffiths, M.A.

pearlpublications.co.uk
Contact: info@pearlpublications.co.uk

A Pictorial Memoir of B.W. Newton: Supplement to 'A Guide to the Works and Remains of Benjamin Wills Newton'.

Paperback: 978-1-901397-15-4
Hardback: 978-1-901397-16-1

First published 2023.

The moral rights of the author are asserted.
Copyright © 2023 by C.W.H. Griffiths.
All rights reserved. No part of this publication may be reproduced or transmitted in any form or by any means without acknowledgement.

British Library CIP Data available.
BISAC: REF004000; REL108020; BIO018000
We acknowledge with thanks:
- Permission from The John Rylands University Library of the University of Manchester to give extended quotations of items held in the Fry Collection.
- Permission from Tom Chantry to include quotations of items of the original Fry Collection now held by him.
- Permission from the Newfoundland and Labrador Heritage Website to use the image of Ker Baillie Hamilton.
- Permission to include images of iron churches from Nick Thomson of Rural Design Architects (https://www.ruraldesign.co.uk), which images he also supplied.
- Permission from The Box, Plymouth (https://www.theboxplymouth.com/) to include the image of Francis Lane's portrait of Samuel Prideaux Tregelles, which the gallery also supplied.
- The supply of the image of W. Lancelot Holland by Rev Edward Malcolm, from *The Gospel Magazine*, May 1895.
- The cover design by David Legg

If any rights have been inadvertently infringed, the publisher apologises, and asks that the omission be excused. Pearl Publications undertakes to correct any such unintentional oversight in subsequent printings.

PREFACE

It was originally intended to include the material in this book in the main volume of the *Guide to the Works and Remains of B.W. Newton*. It is essentially a supplement to that work and consequently has shortcomings in terms of written detail and background which are given in full in the larger work.

The cost of incorporating coloured pictures and graphics into the Guide would have greatly multiplied its production cost. It has been a constant objective to avoid excess cost to those who have an interest in B.W. Newton and his work and therefore it has been published separately.

I nevertheless hope that the issuing of this short supplement will add a human face to what has been written in the *Guide*. These are the people who wrote, preached, and laboured for truths that they held more dearly than life itself.

Most of the items in this *Supplement* are held by C.W.H. Griffiths. All are used by permission.

Chris W.H. Griffiths
September 2023

CONTENTS

Introduction 1

Family Portraits 3

Manuscript material by B.W. Newton 11

Meetings 21

B.W. Newton's death 25

Examples of F.W. Wyatt's copies and notes 29

B.W. Newton's associates 37

    Alfred C. Fry and the 'Fry Manuscript'
    Frederick W. Wyatt
    W. Lancelot Holland
    John Adams
    Thomas Graham Graham and Jane Graham
    Ker Baillie Hamilton
    William Edward Burnett
    George T. Hunt
    Charles T. Walrond

Advertisement for *'The Guide'* 40

INTRODUCTION

The will of B.W. Newton's widow refers to "pictures, miniatures and photographs"[1]. Sadly, no nineteenth century photographs are known to have survived. B.W. Newton eschewed what he perceived as the vanity of pictures of himself.

In terms of portraits, this appendix is, of course, incomplete. None have been found for certain key figures in B.W. Newton's life. Some may have shared his dislike of pictures of themselves. The absence of a picture of John Cox (jnr.), even from his obituary in the magazine he edited, suggests this. Had this appendix been compiled a century ago, it would no doubt have been much fuller.

There are many who we would have liked to have included. To name a few: his mother, Amy Toulmin, Rev John Cox, John Cox (jnr.), Lucas Collins, the Stirling family, the Riach family, Dr A.J.W. Dalzell, and Jane Thornton Daniels (who was largely responsible for the manuscripts posthumously published by Hunt Barnard).

B.W. Newton was a central figure in the beginnings of what became 'the Brethren Movement' in Plymouth. His departure from both Plymouth and the Brethren is the focus of much that has been written of him. He was the target of written attacks from 'the Brethren' throughout his long life, although for more than fifty years he ministered in complete separation from the Brethren. We have not included in this supplement his opponents within the Brethren Movement, nor of his erstwhile supporters before he left it. Portraits and biographical notes regarding many of these are in Henry Pickering's *Chief Men among the Brethren*.

Likewise we have not included other nineteenth century Christian leaders with whom he at various times had friendly relations, such as Horatius Bonar, Professor Smeaton, Lord Litchfield, Pastor Frank White, Dr C.Y. Biss and others.

We have restricted ourselves to co-workers closely associated with B.W. Newton in his main life's work. It is beyond the scope of this supplement or the *Guide* itself to give to give extended biographies of the individuals whose portraits are given. Very interesting biographies could be written of both W. Lancelot Holland and Ker Baillie Hamilton.

Pearl Publications hopes to publish at least two further books regarding B.W. Newton and his associates. These (D.V.) will be:

Regarding the work associated with B.W. Newton in Worthing

Regarding Dr A.J.W. Dalzell, who was B.W. Newton's physician in his last days. He led a group of B.W. Newton's associates who emigrated to Australia and formed a community there. He subsequently died in Jerusalem.

---

[1] See *A Guide to the works and remains of B.W. Newton*, Section 12, Miscellaneous Biographical Items, E5, for a note regarding Mrs Newton's will.

FAMILY PORTRAITS

B.W. Newton as a Young Man

The writing on the reverse of this miniature is 'Believed to be Benjamin Wills Newton the Expositor'. There is no reason to doubt that it is of B.W. Newton. The miniatures were left in Mrs Newton's will to her trustees. Mrs Newton would have had no need to identify the subject, and Newton's associates, who would not have known him as a young man, would have been bound to exercise caution, hence the note.

C.W.H. Griffiths obtained a photographic copy of the miniature in 1988, when it was in possession of Mrs L.I. Fry, daughter-in-law of A.C. Fry (B.W. Newton's colporteur) and he provided a copy of that to the Christian Brethren Archive of the John Ryland Library of the University of Manchester (CBA).

The miniature was later donated to the CBA by Mrs Stewart, the daughter of Mrs L.I. Fry in 2002.[2]

[2] See the *Guide* Section 12, Miscellaneous Biographical Items: B. Pictures.

Sketch of B.W. Newton, aged about 75

B.W. Newton was averse to having his portrait painted or his photograph taken. This 'sketch by Mr Penstone' was referred to in *Perilous Times* in April 1902 with the caution 'The portrait was sketched by the artist twenty years ago, and does not, therefore, represent Mr Newton as his friends knew him at the close of his life'. Edward Penstone also owned the copyright of the widely used portrait of J.N. Darby, which was included in W.B. Neatby, *History of the Plymouth Brethren* (1902).

The Hawkins sisters

B.W. Newton was married to Maria Hawkins. Her spinster sister, Sophia, lived in their household for many years, and led the Sunday School work on the Isle of Wight when B.W. Newton lived there.

C.W.H. Griffiths obtained a photographic copy of these miniatures in 1988, whilst they were in the possession of Mrs L.I. Fry. The miniatures were donated to the CBA by Mrs Stewart, her daughter in 2002.

It is regrettably unknown which of the portraits was B.W. Newton's wife, or even whether the pictures were painted at the same time. It is possible that the removal of the backing of the frames would reveal this. Mrs Maria Newton was 6 years older than her sister, Sophia. Neither of the sisters wears a wedding ring in the portraits. Maria's marriage to Mr Newton was in 1849. In that year Maria would have been 34 and Sophia 28.[3]

---

[3] See the *Guide* Section 12, Miscellaneous Biographical Items: B. Pictures.

Family Portraits

B.W. Newton's Father

Benjamin Wills Newton of Plymouth Dock (B.W. Newton senior) died eleven days before his son's birth, in 1807. B.W. Newton, jun. was his only child. In his early years B.W. Newton, junior, was brought up by his grandparents.

A photographic copy of this miniature was obtained by C.W.H. Griffiths in 1988, when it was in the possession of Mrs L.I. Fry, daughter-in-law of A.C. Fry. A copy is held in the Christian Brethren Archive.

This miniature was in a gold frame and was sold at auction on the Isle of Wight to persons unknown in 2002 by Mrs L.I. Fry's daughter. It was resold by Bonham's of London in 2007.

At its auction by Bonham's the miniature painting was attributed to Soloman Polack (Flemish, 1757-1839).

The back of the frame is also shown below. It contains a lock of hair. [4]

---

[4] See the *Guide* Section 12, Miscellaneous Biographical Items: B. Pictures, for further information regarding its provenance.

Samuel Prideaux Tregelles

S.P. Tregelles was the cousin of B.W. Newton's first wife (née Hannah Abbott). He was his constant associate and correspondent, although there was nearly a breach between them in 1851.[5] B.W. Newton supported his labours to produce a Greek Testament based on the most ancient texts.

The portrait of him below has been widely reproduced, including in G.H. Fromow, *B.W. Newton and Dr S.P. Tregelles: Teachers of the Faith and the Future*. The date and location of the original portrait is unknown.

---

[5] See CBA 7064 p142 and T.C.F. Stunt, *Life and Times of Samuel Prideaux Tregelles*.

This second portrait of S.P. Tregelles is by Francis Lane. It is dated 1860, when Tregelles would have been 47. The original painting is held by The Box gallery in Plymouth.

MANUSCRIPT MATERIAL BY B.W. NEWTON

B.W. Newton's First Book

The copy below was obtained when the book was in the possession of Edwin Cross. The handwriting is unknown, but may have been of B.W. Newton and of one of his grandparents

The book was *Grammatical Institutes, or an Easy Introduction to Dr Lowth's English Grammar, designed for use of Schools and to lead Young Gentlemen and Ladies into the Knowledge of the first Principles of the English Language* by John Ash, LLD., 1807.

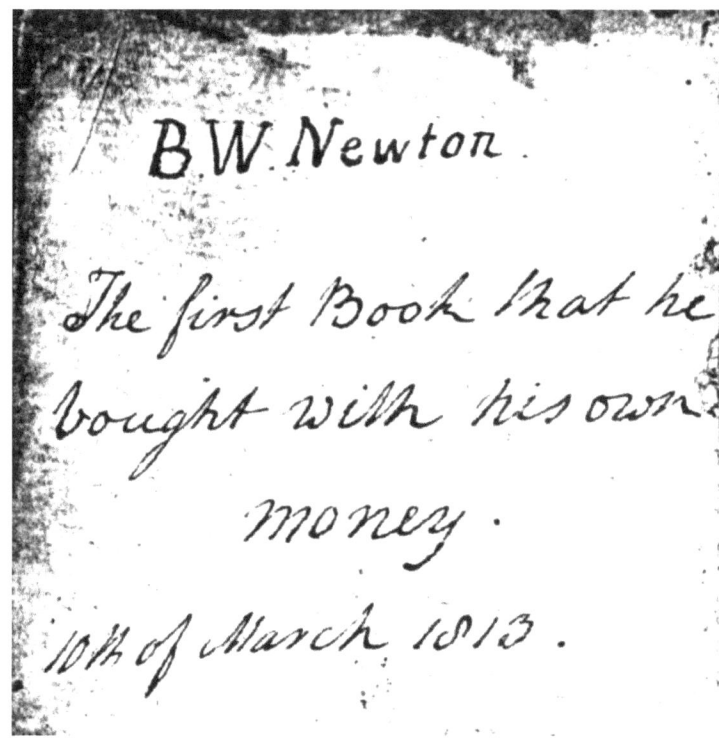

B.W. Newton's Greek New Testament

This Greek New Testament has B.W. Newton's name and the date '1842' in his own handwriting on the inside cover,. C.W.H. Griffiths holds this item, which he obtained from T.C.F. Stunt. For comment on the amendments made by him in the Testament see the *Guide* Section 12, Miscellaneous Biographical Items A.9: Personal Greek New Testament.

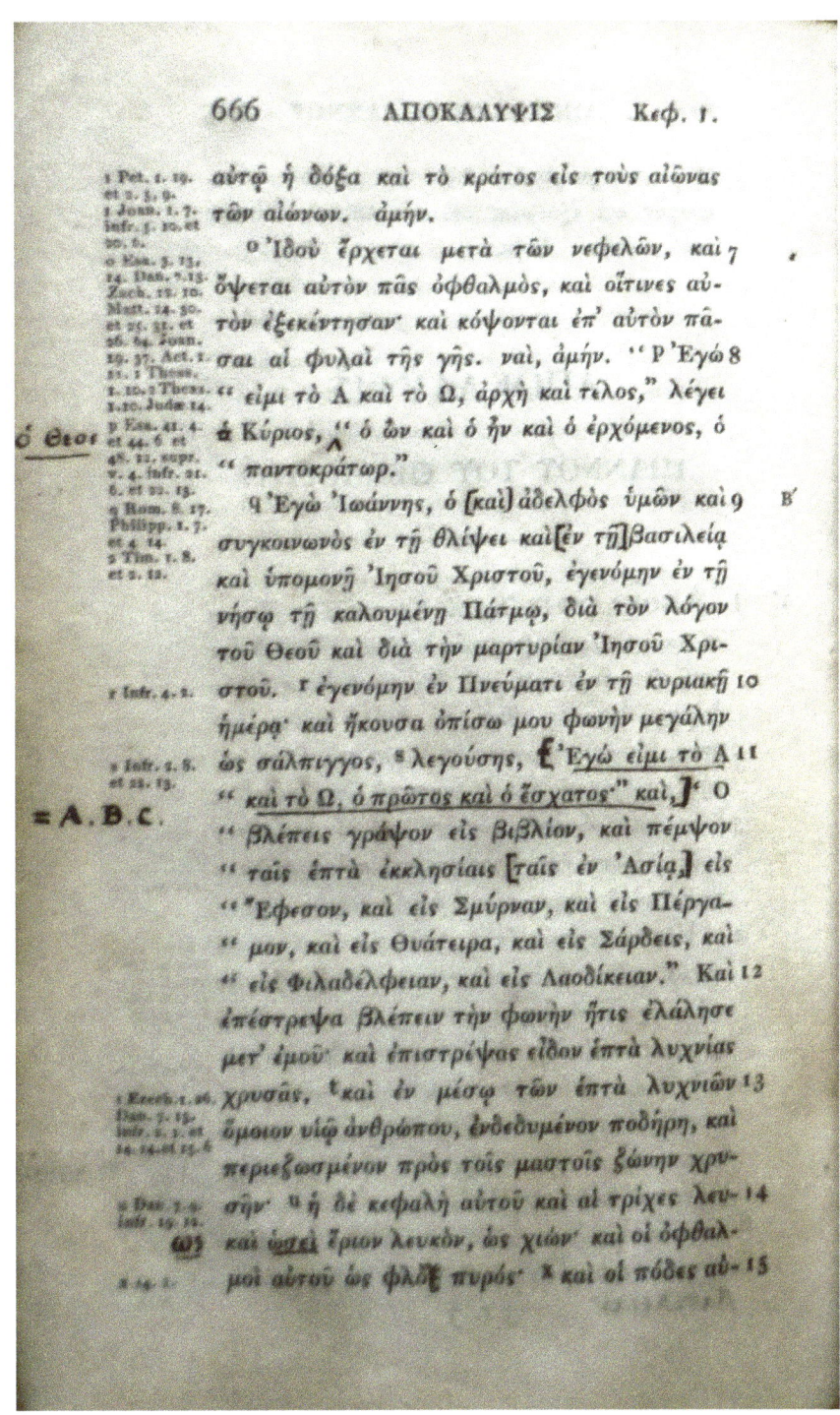

Κεφ. 2.   ΙΩΑΝΝΟΥ.

τοῦ ὅμοιοι χαλκολιβάνῳ, ὡς ἐν καμίνῳ πεπυ-
ρωμένοι· καὶ ἡ φωνὴ αὐτοῦ ὡς φωνὴ ὑδάτων
16 πολλῶν· ʸ καὶ ἔχων ἐν τῇ δεξιᾷ αὐτοῦ χειρὶ
ἀστέρας ἑπτά· καὶ ἐκ τοῦ στόματος αὐτοῦ
ῥομφαία δίστομος ὀξεῖα ἐκπορευομένη· καὶ ἡ
ὄψις αὐτοῦ, ὡς ὁ ἥλιος φαίνει ἐν τῇ δυνάμει
17 αὐτοῦ. ᶻ Καὶ ὅτε εἶδον αὐτὸν, ἔπεσα πρὸς
τοὺς πόδας αὐτοῦ ὡς νεκρός· καὶ ἔθηκε τὴν
δεξιὰν αὐτοῦ [χεῖρα] ἐπ᾽ ἐμὲ, λέγων μοι, "Μὴ
" φοβοῦ. ἐγώ εἰμι ὁ πρῶτος καὶ ὁ ἔσχατος,
18 " ᵃ καὶ ὁ ζῶν, καὶ ἐγενόμην νεκρὸς, καὶ ἰδοὺ
" ζῶν εἰμι εἰς τοὺς αἰῶνας τῶν αἰώνων ἀμήν·
" καὶ ἔχω τὰς κλεῖς τοῦ ᾅδου καὶ τοῦ θανά-
19 " του. Γράψον ἃ εἶδες, καὶ ἅ εἰσι, καὶ ἃ
20 " μέλλει γίνεσθαι μετὰ ταῦτα· ᵇ τὸ μυστή-
" ριον τῶν ἑπτὰ ἀστέρων ὧν εἶδες ἐπὶ τῆς
" δεξιᾶς μου, καὶ τὰς ἑπτὰ λυχνίας τὰς χρυ-
" σᾶς. οἱ ἑπτὰ ἀστέρες, ἄγγελοι τῶν ἑπτὰ
" ἐκκλησιῶν εἰσι· καὶ αἱ ἑπτὰ λυχνίαι [ἃς εἶ-
" δες] ἑπτὰ ἐκκλησίαι εἰσί.

2 " ᶜ ΤΩι ἀγγέλῳ τῆς Ἐφεσίνης ἐκκλησίας   ἐν Ἐφέσῳ
" γράψον, Τάδε λέγει ὁ κρατῶν τοὺς ἑπτὰ
" ἀστέρας ἐν τῇ δεξιᾷ αὐτοῦ, ὁ περιπατῶν ἐν
" μέσῳ τῶν ἑπτὰ λυχνιῶν τῶν χρυσῶν·
2 " ᵈ Οἶδα τὰ ἔργα σου, καὶ τὸν κόπον σου,
" καὶ τὴν ὑπομονήν σου, καὶ ὅτι οὐ δύνῃ βα-
" στάσαι κακούς, καὶ ἐπείρασω τοὺς φάσκον-   λεγοντας ἑαυ-
" τας εἶναι ἀποστόλους, καὶ οὐκ εἰσὶ, καὶ εὗ-   τους ἀποστο-
3 " ρες αὐτοὺς ψευδεῖς, καὶ ἐβάστασας καὶ   λους ειναι
" ὑπομονὴν ἔχεις, καὶ διὰ τὸ ὄνομά μου κεκο-
4 " πίακας καὶ οὐ κέκμηκας. Ἀλλ᾽ ἔχω κατὰ

Example 1 of B.W. Newton's editing for a new edition

This is the First Edition of *Thoughts on the Apocalypse*. The notes are on chapter 14. These notes were incorporated into the second edition. The copy used belonged to Maria Hawkins, prior to her marriage to Mr Newton. Her maiden name in her own hand is written at the front of the book

The original held by C.W.H. Griffiths obtained from Dr Ulrich Bister.

> 190
>
> the oppressed and of the prisoner;—to lay the foundation of his greatness in the miseries and sins of men, and to draw the halo of glory around his single brow, is the object of Antichrist. He comes from beneath—his origin is from the pit (chap. xi. 7). And yet he says, "I will ascend into heaven, I will exalt my throne above the stars of God; I will sit also upon the mount of the congregation, in the sides of the north; I will ascend above the heights of the clouds; I will be like the Most High." ~~But Jesus, not seeking His own, but another's glory, came into the midst of this living mass of corruption and suffering, that He might find in it for Himself sorrow and death—but that He might be to others life.~~ The acuteness of His sensibilities, and the liveliness of His sympathy, which were necessary to His perfectness as man (for it pertains to man to feel), added poignancy to His sufferings. They made Him like a tender plant, beneath a rude and inclement sky. But He lived not for Himself—He came "not to be ministered unto, but to minister, and to give His life a ransom for many." His life has been taken from the earth; but His memorial is blessed for ever. And when the time shall come for Him to return from the pavilion of God, in which He is now hidden, and to stand upon Zion in possession of the government of earth, it will be as no unknown stranger, but as One who has been known, and proved, and found worthy—known in His eternal glory before the world was—known in suffering and in death—known in the present exercise of the
>
> ** But Jesus whose home was in the Father's glory, seeking Another's glory & others blessing, came into this living mass of corruption & suffering to find in it for Himself ... & death*

little, I mean, in comparison with that hour when all things shall be heard giving thanks because He shall have opened His hand to satisfy the desire of every living thing.

power of the Almighty throne. He has been known by God, known by the Spirit of God also in His saints, and we are able to say that "He is worthy."

The purpose of the Lamb in again visiting the earth, is to bring into it, and finally to establish in it, the glory and the holiness, and the happiness of heaven. He has finished the work of atonement, and has sat down on the throne of the majesty in the heavens; but we wait for His return, in order that we may behold what the full manifested results of redemption are to be. The love which God hath to us, is at present little evidenced by the things around us, ~~which the eye seeth~~ *(see top of page)*. We know *His love* inwardly;—it is "shed abroad in our hearts, through the holy Spirit," and inwardly we are comforted and strengthened. To our hearts secretly it is like dew upon the thirsty ground, or like ointment poured upon the burning wound. But these effects are hidden. They are secret in the heart; whilst every thing around us groans; and we ourselves in unredeemed bodies, eat our bread with the sweat of our brow, from a ground that the Lord hath cursed. ~~So that~~ *Thus* to the Spirit, it still is what it was to Jesus, the valley of the shadow of death, and all the fires that men kindle, that they may warm themselves in the sparks of their kindling, and say, "Aha, I am warm, I have seen the fire," only add, to the eye of faith, new ~~horrors~~ *terrors* to the scene. *Nevertheless* ~~Yet~~ it is in this world, that the glory and holiness, and happiness of heaven, is to be manifested, and established. *Finally*, its establishment will

a death, that He might be to others life.

Example 2 of B.W. Newton's editing for a new edition

This is from an unpublished revision of *Occasional Papers on Scriptural Subjects*

The original is held by C.W.H. Griffiths and was obtained from Dr Ulrich Bister.

NOTES ON THE WORDS Λογιζομαι, &c.

when their progenitor sinned. The very subject, therefore, of the passage, is "imputed sin" in the theological sense of "imputed": and therefore if there be any passage in the Bible from which "impute," *in the other sense*, ought to be excluded, it is this. The use of this word was, no doubt an oversight on the part of the Translators but the Revisers who have had time to canvass all that has been said & written on the subject, have not seen fit to rectify the error.

But we have not only to distinguish between ελλογεω and λογιζομαι, (whether used transitively as Rom. iv. 6, "Even as David describeth the blessedness of the man to whom the Lord imputeth righteousness without works"—λογιζεται δικαιοσυνην χωρις εργων: or intransitively as in Rom. iv. 11, "that righteousness might be imputed unto them also"—εις το λογισθηναι και αυτοις την δικαιοσυνην) is *also* to be distinguished from λογιζομαι ΕΙΣ, in the sense in which λογιζομαι ΕΙΣ is used in the fourth of Romans. I say *as used in the fourth of Romans*, because in determining the specific meaning of words, we have to consider not merely what they *may* mean in other combinations, but what they mean as limited and defined by the context in which they occur. Both in the second and fourth of Romans, λογιζομαι in combination with ΕΙΣ, is evidently used to denote the assigning to a thing a value which intrinsically it has not. Thus in Rom. ii., "Shall not his uncircumcision be counted FOR circumcision?" (ουχι η ακροβυστια αυτου εις περιτομην λογισθησεται); and in Rom. iv., "His faith is counted FOR righteousness" (λογιζεται η πιστις αυτου εις δικαιοσυνην)—that is, faith has assigned to it a value which intrinsically it has not, for our faith is not in itself righteousness. It is neither perfect in its development, nor meritorious; nor is it regarded as a work at all, but on the contrary, is contrasted with works—"to him that worketh not, but believeth."

If I were to endow another with ten thousand talents of gold, and were to give him, in proof of his being so endowed, a legally stamped document—that document would become possessed of a conventional value, and might be reckoned to me for the value of the talents which it denoted; but it would have no intrinsic value. In such a case I should use the expression λογιζομαι ΕΙΣ. So is it with faith. It is not, as Romanists and others have said, righteousness. It has only an assigned value: whereas, Christ's righteousness which it represents, and on account of which it has its assigned value, has a real, absolute, value. *It* is as the true gold, whereas faith is only as the stamped document. Consequently, I say faith is imputed to me *for* righteousness; but of Christ's righteousness I say, it is imputed to me *as* righteousness. Faith imputed *for* righteousness, and the

Example of B.W. Newton's Letter writing

This is a copy of a letter in his own hand to Mrs Riach on the first anniversary of the death of her husband, 7th February 1866. The Riachs were staunch supporters of B.W. Newton from the early years of his separation from the Brethren until his old age.

Recovered from the Stirling Collection by C.W.H. Griffiths. The original is now at the CBA

> My dear Mrs Riach
>
> I accept with thankfulness the kind present you have sent me, which I shall value on every account; but especially as being a memorial of one whose faithful friendship & affection were to me thro' a long series of sorrowful years a peculiar source of comfort & encouragement. The void caused by his removal I still feel and always expect to feel. Therefore I can well understand your sorrow. But we must strive to look onward not backward: for the

Retrospect is too painful. Hope has to do with the future not with the past. I am sure you strive to do this, altho' it may sometimes be very difficult. Yet you have hitherto been sustained from day to day and the end cannot be very far distant, when sorrow now known, but then past for ever, will only by their remembrance, heighten present joy.

Accept the assurance of my most true sympathy & believe me
My dear Mrs Reed
Yours in sincerest Christian sympathy
B W Newton

Feby 7th 1866

MEETINGS

MEETINGS

Meeting places

When he moved to Bayswater, London, after leaving the Brethren, B.W. Newton commenced a work at 'Duke Street Chapel', Bayswater. By 1960 he was meeting in what the Daily Telegraph described as 'a commodious iron church'[6] in Queens Road, St James's Park. When his work in London ended, the premises were sold to a coach maker, but the chapel was demolished as he was concerned that the

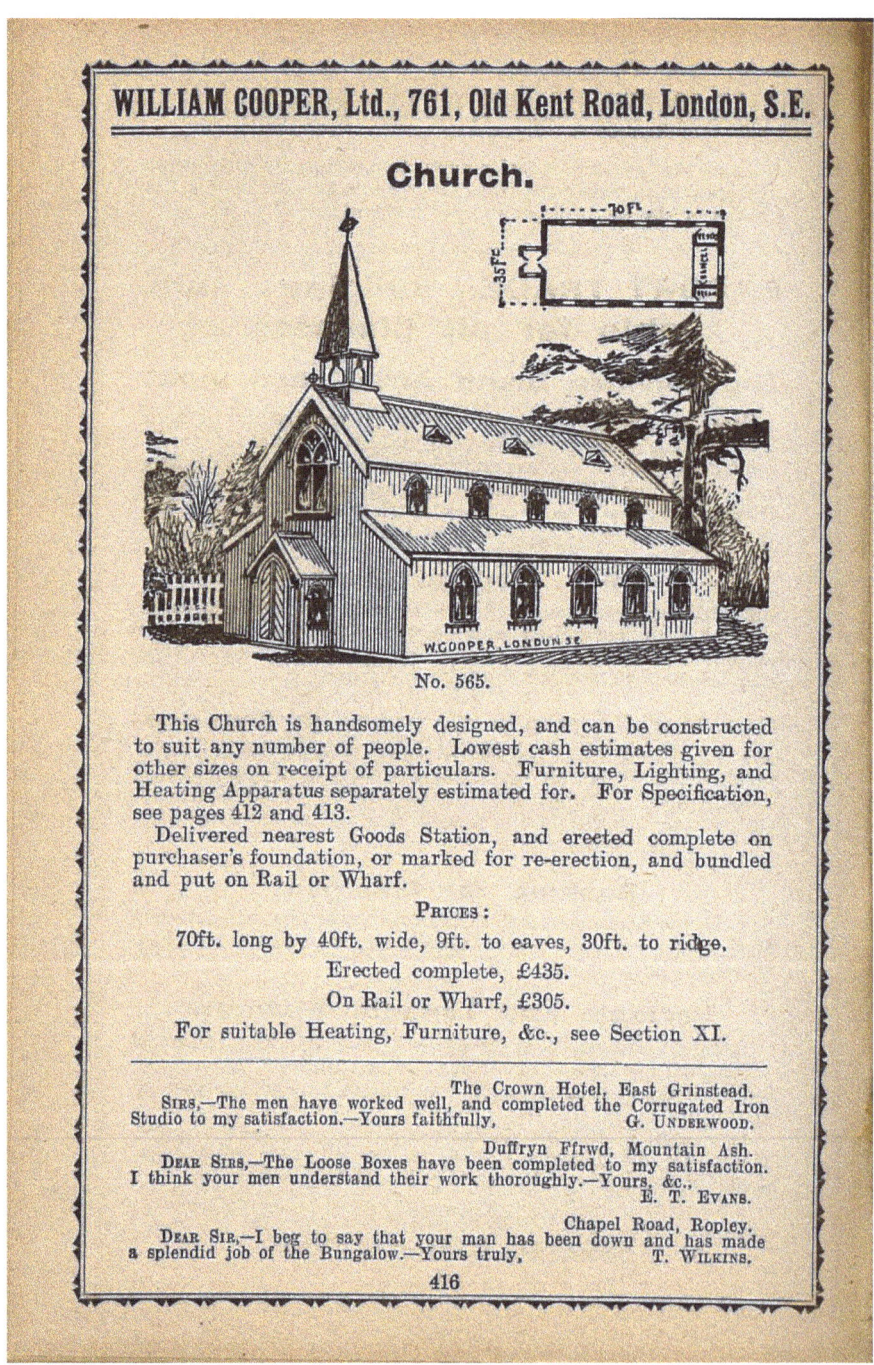

---

[6] 'Mr Newton at Bayswater', Daily Telegraph, 24th May 1870

building might fall into the hands of ritualists or Roman Catholics.[7]

These iron churches, or, as they were nicknamed, 'tin tabernacles' were popular in the nineteenth century. C.H. Spurgeon raised money for them to be exported to the far corners of the British Empire, including Stanley in the Falkland Islands.

The illustrations show the type of building B.W. Newton evidently used. The images are used courtesy of Nick Thomson of Rural Design Architects (https://www.ruraldesign.co.uk)

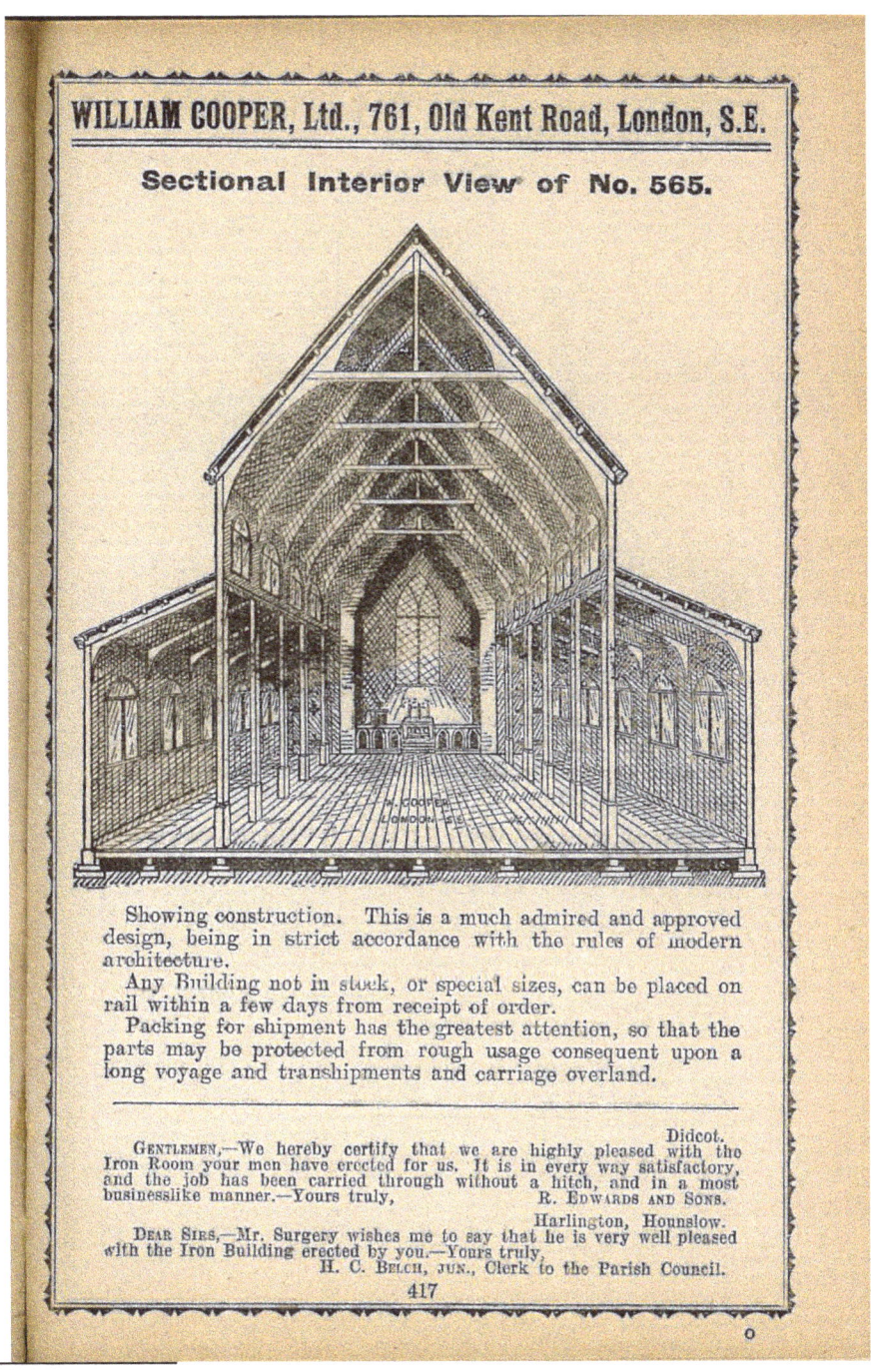

---

[7] See the Fry Collection, CBA 7050 p.74

Notices of meetings

Notice of Duke Street Meetings, 1st June 1857.

From *The Times*.

> LECTURES at DUKE-STREET CHAPEL, St. James's-park, (entrance near Storey's-gate.)—The following Lectures will be given (D.V.):—
> To-morrow Evening, June 2, at 7 o'clock.—General Scope of the Book of Revelation.
> Sunday Evening, June 7, at half-past 6.—The Scripture Doctrine of Baptism.   BENJAMIN WILLS NEWTON.
> Dated June 1, 1857.

Notice of Meetings arranged at Great Marlborough Street, 28th March 1878.

From *The Times*.

> BENJAMIN WILLS NEWTON will LECTURE on Prophetic Scripture every consecutive Thursday, at 11.30, until further notice, at the Rooms of the Christian Young Men's Association, 48, Great Marlborough-street, Regent-street.

Notice of meetings arranged at Stafford Rooms Y.M.C.A, 10th May 1887.

Copy in CBA - 7188(1)[8]

> **LECTURES AT THE STAFFORD ROOMS.**
>
> Mr. B. W. Newton proposes (D.V.) to give a few Lectures on PROPHETIC AND OTHER PARTS OF SCRIPTURE, at the Stafford Rooms, Titchborne St., Edgware Road, on consecutive Tuesday Mornings at a Quarter-past Eleven o'clock.
>
> The first Lecture to be on Tuesday, May 10th.
>
> LONDON, May, 1887.

---

[8] For further information about Stafford Rooms, and the messages that were delivered there see *The Guide to the Works and Remains of B.W. Newton'*

B.W. NEWTON'S DEATH

Note in Mrs Stirling's book

What has been called 'the Stirling Collection' was recovered from the library of Spurgeon's College to the Christian Brethren Archive in 1995. It included two bound sets of B.W. Newton's works with some rare items, for example, several in German, together with manuscript copies of items and letters. She and her husband were close associates of B.W. Newton and corresponded with him in his final years. See the correspondence and the note on the Stirling Collection in Section 10 of the *Guide*.

> Mary E. Stirling.
> From Benjamin Wills Newton
> The Author
> May 19th 1899.
> Our beloved & revered Friend
> died June 26. 1899. 1.a.m.
> aged 91.
> at 2. Clanricarde Gardens
> Tunbridge Wells.
> as he wished - alone -

THOUGHTS

ON

PARTS OF THE PROPHECY OF

ISAIAH.

In Memoriam Card

This was produced just after B.W. Newton's death. See further note in *the Guide,* Section 12 Miscellaneous Biographical Items, E Items relating to his death.

IN MEMORY OF
BENJAMIN WILLS NEWTON,

Born December 12th, 1807, and entered into his rest June 26th, 1899.

Amidst bitter opposition he contended earnestly for the Faith once delivered to the saints: for the ancient truths of the deity and true humanity of the Lord Jesus: for the justification of believers through the blood and righteousness of their God and Saviour, Jesus Christ: and for the unity in glory, as one Church of God, of the redeemed of all ages.

He laboured, too, to unfold the Prophetic Scriptures, and to declare the true character and the doom of this present age, and the right expectancy of the Lord's return.

"Blessed are ye, when men shall hate you, and when they shall separate you from their company, and shall reproach you, and cast out your name as evil, for the Son of man's sake. Rejoice ye in that day, and leap for joy: for behold, your reward is great in heaven: for in the like manner did their fathers unto the prophets." —Luke vi. 22, 23.

Photograph of the gravestone of B.W. Newton and his wife, together with the gravestone of his mother.

See the *Guide*, Section 12, Miscellaneous Biographical Items, E Items Relating to his Death, for further comment on this. .His mother's gravestone is now illegible.

Mrs ANNA NEWTON,
FORMERLY OF LOSTWITHIEL AND PLYMOUTH;
BORN AUGUST 12TH 1782;
DIED JUNE 8TH 1877.

"IN WHOM WE HAVE REDEMPTION THROUGH HIS BLOOD,
EVEN THE FORGIVENESS OF SINS."

"MY HOPE IS BUILT ON NOTHING LESS
THAN JESUS' BLOOD AND RIGHTEOUSNESS;
I DARE NOT TRUST THE SWEETEST FRAME,
BUT WHOLLY LEAN ON JESUS' NAME,
ON CHRIST, THE SOLID ROCK, I STAND,
ALL OTHER GROUND IS SINKING SAND!"

BENJAMIN WILLS NEWTON,
FORMERLY FELLOW OF EXETER COLLEGE, OXFORD,
BORN DECEMBER 12TH 1807,
AND ENTERED INTO HIS REST JUNE 26TH 1899.

THE RESURRECTION MORN WILL BREAK,
AND EVERY SLEEPING SAINT AWAKE,
    CALL'D FORTH TO LIFE AGAIN;
O MORE! TOO BRIGHT FOR MORTAL EYES,
WHEN ALL THE RANSOM'D CHURCH SHALL RISE
AND WING THEIR WAY TO YONDER SKIES,
    CALL'D UP WITH CHRIST TO REIGN.

Also of MARIA NEWTON,
WIFE OF THE ABOVE,
BORN JANUARY 13TH 1815,
DIED DECEMBER 25TH 1909.

F.W. WYATT'S COPIES AND NOTES

F.W. Wyatt was B.W. Newton's constant associate in his last days. He was his amanuensis when his sight failed. F.W. Wyatt's meticulous transcription of important documents and accounts of meetings form the bulk of the 'Fry Collection'.

Example of Letter Transcription

This letter of B.W. Newton to Dr Luigi Desanctis is in Wyatt's MS Book 1 pp.359-361. It illustrates the clarity of his writing and style, and his close attention to detail. The content of the letter is of considerable interest.

> The two following should be placed next after the letter of April 15. being enclosures with it.
>
> Copy of BW Newton's letter to De Sanctis.
>
> 70 New Finchley Road
> April 5th 1864
>
> My dear Dr Desanctis
>   I cannot for a moment suppose that it is your desire to give me pain or to do me injustice. — On the contrary, I have always supposed that you have sympathised with me under the misrepresentations and false insinuations of a party of whose bitterness & violence you too have had some experience. — I must however own to you that I have been considerably surprised & distressed at observing in a paper you have recently published the following sentences:

"Will the author or authors exclude from Christianity
"the Darbyites who are a part of the Plymouthists?
"They exclude the Newtonians who are another part
"of them. The Darbyites have a lay-papacy,
"the Newtonians have errors & heresies."

   Observe, you have not said "the New=
tonians are represented as having errors & heresies":
but have used a form of expression that would
lead persons to suppose that you acquiesce in the
statement that the Newtonians have errors & heresies.

   Secondly, your words imply that I am con=
nected with the "Plymouthists"—in fact that my=
self & friends are a section of them. I thought
that you had been aware that neither myself in Lon=
don, nor Dr Tregelles in Plymouth, are or have been
for the last sixteen years & more connected with
those denominated "Brethren" or "Plymouthists."
We have nothing to do with them or any of their
sections. Dr Tregelles is elder in a congregation
called a "free evangelical church", having for its pastor
the Rev: William Elliott, a minister recommended
as pastor to that church by Mr Baptist Noel & others.
whilst I am, according to the law of my country,
legally registered as the minister of a "congregation
of Protestants holding the Creeds & first eighteen
Articles of the Church of England, but rejecting her
orders & ritual." I have a Chapel in which I regu=
larly preach & lecture, of which I am the sole min=
ister; neither adopting the order nor holding the doc=
trines of the "Brethren." Indeed, there are no two per=
sons in the world who have been more resolutely &
consistently opposed to the distinctive doctrines of the
"Brethren" for the last thirty years & more than Dr

Tregelles & myself. I send you a tract recently published by Dr Tregelles in which you will see his sentiments.

I have believed, and still do believe, that in all the great foundation doctrines of our holy faith my views are in strict (sic) with your own. I take it for granted that you do <u>not</u> hold with many of the "Brethren" that the Lord Jesus had a "heavenly humanity" — that you strictly hold the doctrines expressed in the Scotch & English Confessions on that & kindred subjects — that you do <u>not</u> reject the doctrine of the imputed righteousness of our Lord & Saviour — that you utterly reject the fearful system introduced among the "Brethren" of explaining a large portion of the New Testament as "Jewish" and not properly Christian — that you believe that the Church in glory will include, not a section of the redeemed, but all the redeemed — that you admit that the ministry of pastors (recognised) & teachers is an abiding ordinance in the church. On these & similar points, you are to the best of my belief in strict accordance with Dr Tregelles & myself.

I may add that in past years when an attempt was made in England to excite a strong feeling against yourself at the time you left the Vaudois, I always endeavoured, whenever I had the opportunity, to vindicate your course and to shew that you did not really sanction the ministerial principles & order of the "Brethren" though for a time you might seem to be identified with them, especially as respected the order of your morning meetings.

As regards the "Brethren" they really are divided

only into two sections — Darbyite Brethren & non-Darbyite; and as to <u>doctrine</u> (and this is most important to observe) they are not divided at all. All their peculiarities of doctrine & practice are traceable to Mr Darby who is, virtually, master of them all.. Indeed I scarcely know one amongst them who can be said to have an independent judgment. They are like sheep who, having been introduced by their master into a wide plain, wish to wander about in it apart from the control of him who brought them there; & the master not approving of this, there has been rebellion & strife.

As regards the appellation "Newtonian" I beg to observe that it is altogether inappropriate.. I carefully avoid anything that would tend to make me the leader of a party. Every one who is recognised as a believer is welcomed at the Lord's Table in Bayswater Chapel whenever he pleases to come.— He is not required to attach to me or to my teaching or to renounce membership in any body to which he may happen to belong. It is evidently impossible that a sect could be formed on such principles. Consequently I cannot but feel that I am injuriously treated in being represented as acting on like principles with the Darbyites, who have in print styled themselves "the one assembly of God in London." Your observations having been printed in a periodical & extensively circulated in this country are calculated to do me much harm, & of course considerably add to the difficulties which false representations from the "Brethren" have already caused me.

I send by Book Post two parcels. If you will be so good as to look at the end of "Occasional Papers", which is my last publication, you will there see a list of all my published works. My sentiments & doctrines are in them fully expressed, & if you can point out any _heresy_ in them I will not refuse, on its being shewn me, to make recantation. You will not expect _perfectness_ in any human work. There is none perfect but One.

If you should happen to see Dr Horatius Bonar who, I believe, is now in Italy, I should be obliged by your shewing him this note, and asking him to explain to you my relation to the "Brethren" or rather non-relation.

I can assure you that it gave me great pain some years ago to think of the near relation in which you seemed to stand to the "Brethren"; & it was my earnest desire that you might be caused in some way to take a separate & independent stand as a minister of Christ.

I enclose an extract from a letter I wrote some months ago to a clergyman who was under the impression that I was connected with the "Brethren". I enclose it because I have expressed myself somewhat more fully respecting their peculiar doctrines than I have in my present letter.

I remain, dear Dr Desanctis, Yours very truly
B. W. Newton.

ENCLOSURE

Copy of extract of letter written to a clergyman by BW Newton. Nov 1863

My dear Sir

* * * I observe in your note that you suppose I am in connexion with the "Plymouth Brethren". This is a mistake that I am exceedingly anxious to

Example of F.W. Wyatt's Notes

Notes on the Quakers and B.W. Newton's relatedness to Samuel Lloyd. The original is now held by Tom Chantry.

"About 1836 a great wave of controversy passed over English Friends. The result was that in Manchester monthly meeting alone, fifty heads of families and one hundred and fifty leading members resigned their membership, and thus the Society lost many of its brightest ornaments. [Some few years before, many Friends in England and large numbers in America had left the Society, to follow a new leader, Elias Hicks, a man of Unitarian & Pantheistic views. See for a full account "The Inner Life of the Religious Societies of the Commonwealth." by Robt Barclay].

Samuel Lloyd was one of those who left. He was baptised, and he & his son Sampson Lloyd (who was first cousin by marriage to BWN's mother) attended & chiefly sustained a meeting of Brethren, in Waterloo St. Birmingham.—" "Farm & its Inhabitants" page 73.

This Samuel Lloyd was born 1768, died Nov 10 1849 aged 81. He & Rachel his wife had twelve children, of whom the third (named also *Samuel*) married Mary Honeychurch, first cousin to B.W.N's mother, and aunt to Miss Toulmin.—

Miss Toulmin gives the relationship thus:

```
                        Roger Treffry =
                            |
                 ┌──────────┴──────────┐
                 │ (Eleven in issue)    │
Mary Veale = Roger Treffry         Jane Treffry = Joseph Honeychurch
        |                                      |
   ┌────┴────┐                        ┌────────┴────────┐
Benj W. Newton = Anna Treffry    Mary Honeychurch = Samuel Lloyd    Amy Honeychurch
The Elder       (eleven in issue)                                   = married Toulmin
                buried at Tunbr.Wells                                      |
        |                              |                            Miss Toulmin & a brother
   Benj. Wills Newton              nine children
   died at Tunbr. Wells
```

"Both Roger Treffry's had issue 8 sons & 3 daughters.—

B.W. NEWTON'S ASSOCIATES

Alfred C. Fry

Frederick W. Wyatt

W. Lancelot Holland

John Adams

Thomas Graham Graham and Jane Graham

Ker Baillie Hamilton

William Edward Burnett

George T. Hunt

Charles T. Walrond

Alfred Charles Fry (1869-1943)

A.C. Fry was employed as a colporteur by B.W. Newton on the Isle of Wight, where he was later an evangelist and children's worker, funded by a legacy from B.W. Newton. He had charge of the repository of manuscripts and publications that has become known as 'The Fry Collection' It was later donated to the Christian Brethren Archive of the John Ryland University Library, Manchester. . He compiled the so-called "Fry Manuscript".[9]

The photograph was provided by his son's, (C.E. Fry's) widow, Grace Fry, to C.W.H. Griffiths. The CBA holds a copy.

---

[9] For further background regarding him, see the *Guide* Section 10 – Duplicated and Manuscript items: Explanatory Note on the Fry Collection.

A.C Fry's Preface to 'The Fry Manuscript'

This M.S. Book contains a collection of interesting things during the lifetime of the late

Benjamin Wills Newton

formerly Fellow of Exeter College in the Oxford University. —

Apart from various letters from his Mother and others, some of which relate to his early experiences with the Plymouth Brethren, most of the things recorded fell from his own lips & pen & were taken down by his friend the late Frederick W. Wyatt (of Blandford, Dorset) in a system of shorthand of his own & copied out more fully by him in his old age. He spent much of his life with B.W.N. —

I have taken most of the things mentioned from F.W. Wyatt's M.S. Books & put them up together as near as I could according to their dates. Many things which I have underlined - especially names of Persons - are simply that they may the more readily be traced whilst reading. There is no thought in this Book of preparing for publishing, but only collecting of material that it might not be lost. — If someone more skilful than myself ever wished to publish that noble gentleman's life story they will find here much useful matter. —

Alfred C. Fry.

Frederick William Wyatt (1842-1933)

F.W. Wyatt was a private secretary to, and close associate of, B.W. Newton at the end of his life. He wrote and transcribed most of the notebooks in the Fry Collection.[10]

The following note is extracted from the *Guide*

"Frederick William Wyatt (3rd March 1842-1933), was born, christened, and spent his childhood in Romsey, Hampshire, with his brother Alfred and his younger sister. He was a watchmaker by trade, as was possibly his father. He first met B.W. Newton in 1875-1877 during B.W. Newton's 'seclusion' in Winchester. He wrote to B.W. Newton on 21st December 1882, recounting his separation from the Brethren, with whom he was then associated at Blandford. In the letter he considers the possibility of leaving Blandford. He subsequently moved to the Isle of Wight to be near, and later to assist, B.W. Newton. He acted as his private secretary, and as an amanuensis when Mr Newton lost his sight. He resided at Ryde. On the Isle of Wight he formed a close friendship with Alfred C. Fry. After B.W. Newton's death he conducted a ministry in the London suburb of Blackheath. He later resided at Blandford again, and possibly Tunbridge Wells. According to his obituary in *Watching and Waiting*, he became 'feeble minded' in old age."

The photograph on the next page was provided to C.W.H. Griffiths by C.E. Fry.

---

[10] For further background regarding Frederick Wyatt see the *Guide* Section 10 – Duplicated and Manuscript items: Explanatory Note on the Fry Collection.

Walter Lancelot Holland (1852-1936)

Walter Lancelot Holland, a former episcopal minister, ordained by J.C. Ryle, was an associate of B.W. Newton in the last years of his life. B.W. Newton's discussions with him and others are recorded in F.W. Wyatt's notebooks in the Fry Collection.[11] He was a colourful, somewhat eccentric, character. For reference to him in the *Guide* see Section 8, Derivative Publications, Publications by W. Lancelot Holland.

George Fromow opined to C.W.H. Griffiths that, had Lancelot Holland not subsequently adopted a Seventh Day Sabbath position, he would have most likely provided the leadership of Mr Newton's circle of friends after his death. He wrote a number of books and pamphlets including *The Archbishop of Canterbury and Modern Christianity* (1898). C.W. H. Griffiths holds a number of resources regarding him and met with Ruth Tilling, a childhood member of his congregation in 1998. The picture is from *The Gospel Magazine*, May 1895, which gives a biography to that date.

---

[11] For further background see Section 8, Derivative Publications, Publications by W. Lancelot Holland in the *Guide*.

Thomas Graham Graham (1824-1905) and Jane Graham (1828(?)-1893)

T.G. Graham and Jane Graham for a time attended Mr Newton's meeting in Bayswater. The Grahams both had Cornish connections, and she introduced her husband to Mr Newton. From Paddington they moved to Worthing, where he built New Street Chapel, and organised and funded a network of village chapels and preachers in the surrounding villages. The chapels were termed *Evangelical Protestant* (the nomenclature used of other chapels associated with B.W. Newton). A Protestant Evangelical School and Sunday School were also later founded.

B.W. Newton's mother, as well as Mr Newton and his wife, stayed with him in Worthing. T.G. Graham later travelled to the Isle of Wight with John Adams, pastor of New Street Chapel, to have discussions with B.W. Newton there. John Cox (jun.) was later associated with T.G. Graham and the Worthing work'[12].

Permission to use the portraits on the following pages is courtesy of Harry Graham, his great great grandson. The large portraits passed to his daughter, Harriet who provided these photographic copies, following his death in 2016.

John Adams (1822-1895)

John Adams became pastor of Angmering Chapel in 1847. He appears to have arranged meetings on prophecy at Worthing in 1859, at which both B.W. Newton and Robert Govett spoke. Two tracts by Mr Newton followed, *The Antichrist future*, and *The Twelve Hundred and Sixty Days of Antichrist's Reign Future.* They gave an account of his messages at these meetings, and reply to the historicist teaching that the Rector of Broadwater promoted afterwards.

When Thomas Graham Graham moved to Worthing and built New Street Chapel in 1861, John Adams became its pastor, and ministered there until his death. Along with T.G. Graham, he had discussions with B.W. Newton on the Isle of Wight.

The Worthing Gazette gave a moving account of his funeral and internment, John Cox (jun.) moved to Worthing and gave some help before John Adams died, and enabled the continuance of the testimony to B.W. Newton's teaching at Chatsworth Hall, Worthing. The portrait was downloaded from the former website of Worthing Baptist Church. Regrettably this, the only surviving portrait of John Adams, used for the website, appears to have been lost when the Church Archives were transferred to The Angus Library, Regents Park College, in 2016. The picture was approximately 5x4 or 6x4, and on a white mounting board of about 10x8 (quarto) size. It was probably not framed.

---

[12] See the MS Fry 1/1/1 at the CBA regarding the conversations of Graham, Adams and Wyatt with Mr Newton at Newport, IoW. For further information regarding John Adams and the Worthing work, see *Mr Newton at Worthing*, by C.W.H. Griffiths held by the Worthing Record Office, which Pearl Publications hopes to publish in an enlarged form.

Thomas Graham Graham

Jane Graham

Ker Baillie Hamilton, CB (1804-1889)

Ker Baillie Hamilton entered the Indian military service in 1822. He went on to serve in Mauritius and the Cape of Good Hope. In 1846 he became governor of Grenada. He became the administrator of Barbados and the Windward Islands in 1851. He was then made the Governor of Newfoundland 1852-1855. His last posting was as Governor and Commander-in-Chief over the Islands of Antigua, Montserrat, Barbuda, St. Christopher Nevis, Anguilla, the Virgin Islands, and Dominica, which he held for twelve years. In 1862 when he was awarded the Companion of the Order of Bath for services to the British Empire. See the biographical note regarding him in *Dictionary of Canadian Biography*, Vol. 11 (available online) and reference to his correspondence in the *Guide*.

KER BAILLIE HAMILTON
1852

Following his retirement in 1867, he became a correspondent with, and keen supporter of, B.W. Newton. He produced promotional pamphlets regarding Mr Newton's *Aids to Prophetic Enquiry* and *Prospects of the Ten Kingdoms*. He attended B.W. Newton's meeting in Bayswater and defended B.W. Newton's decision to close his chapel there. He lived and was buried in Tunbridge Wells.

This image was scanned from page 466 of D.W. Prowse's *A History of Newfoundland,*. Prowse's history was first published in 1895. The image is taken "from an old photograph." The original picture was evidently of equally poor quality and is not known to have survived.

William Edward Burnett (1862-1950)

The Burnett family lived in Ryde, Isle of Wight, where W.E. Burnett's father was associated with B.W. Newton. W.E. Burnett met B.W. Newton in 1891 when he was in Newport, and frequently went to see him when he moved to Shanklin. However, much of W.E Burnett's life was spent in China; with the China Inland Mission for ten years, and then with the 'Evangelical Protestant Mission to the Chinese' which he founded in 1893. He died in China, suffering greatly at the hands of the communists as an old man.

The portrait was published with an obituary in *Watching and Waiting* Sept/Oct 1950.

George Turnor Hunt (1855-1936)

G.T. Hunt was a founding editor of *Perilous Times* from 1899 -1919. When the magazine became *Watching and Waiting* in 1919 he continued as an editor of the new title until his death in 1936. His printing press (Hunt, Barnard and Co) produced many tracts and pamphlets from notes of Mr Newton's addresses in the early years of the 20th Century. For further reference to him see the *Guide*, Section 8, Derivative Publications, note regarding Hunt, Barnard and Co. We have no record that he was a personal associate of B.W. Newton, but he was a key member of the circle of his friends when Mr Newton died and did much to circulate his teaching.

The portrait was published with an obituary in *Watching and Waiting*, February 1936.

Charles Troubridge Walrond
(Died 1942, aged 84)

Charles T. Walrond, a civil engineer, was B.W. Newton's principal executor, and trustee of his books and publishing after his death.[13] It is probable that he held bulk of the items in the Fry Collection before transferring them to A.C. Fry.

This photograph was provided to C.W.H. Griffiths by C.E. Fry.

---

[13] For further information regarding him see Section 10, An Explanatory Note on the Fry Collection.

ADVERTISEMENT

A Guide to the Works and Remains of Benjamin Wills Newton

978-1-901397-12-3   Paperback
978-1-901397-13-0   Hardback
978-1-901397-14-7   Ebook

Published by Pearl Publications, September 2023

Available online from Amazon and by order from bookshops.

Strictly speaking, this *Pictorial Memoir* is a part of the *Guide*. It owes its separate existence to the costs associated with colour printing, and the price impact on the larger work if this material was included in it, thereby making it a colour production for printing purposes.

The *Guide* is the product of decades-long research. The resources of more than 200 libraries have been checked. A substantial amount of material has been discovered and recovered.

Benjamin Wills Newton (1807-1899) was a Christian leader and expositor of Cornish heritage. He was the principal leader at Plymouth in the earliest development of what became the 'Plymouth Brethren'. He left the movement in 1848 after a long controversy with John Nelson Darby. For the next 50 years he followed a distinctive course of writing and independent ministry that was valued his lifetime by the Bonar brothers and George Smeaton amongst many others. The clarity of his theological writings was commended by Dr Martyn Lloyd Jones. However, we believe his most notable contribution was to the study and exposition of unfulfilled prophecy.

Part 1 of the Guide includes the following:

1. Full index to the titles of 490 published works by, or ascribed to, B.W. Newton.
2. Bibliography of B.W. Newton's published works indicating pagination, size and location of surviving copies.
3. Listing and description of all known contributions made by B.W. Newton to other publications and periodicals.
4. Evaluation of authorship of anonymous publications variously ascribed to B.W. Newton by detailed analysis of internal and external evidence.
5. Detailed analysis of 28 articles in the first Brethren publication, The Christian Witness, in relation to his possible or proven authorship.
6. A catalogue of publications derived from notes of addresses, and posthumously published letters and manuscripts.

Part 2 of the Guide describes manuscript and typescript material, and ephemera that have survived. This second part therefore consists of:

7. Known correspondence directly relating to B.W. Newton from various sources. This has been summarised and arranged in date order. Where correspondence is held by the Christian Brethren Archive we have given the catalogue numbers.

8. Manuscript and duplicated materials. These are principally, but not exclusively, those originally in 'The Fry Collection'. We have only listed the items in the Fry Collection that are of direct relevance to this Guide. We have given an outline of relevant material in the Archive to show what is available. We have given the remainder of the material not in the CBA in greater detail, insofar as we have been able to access it.

9. Indexes of B.W. Newton's Works. These are (with one exception) in typescript and MS. They represent early attempts to index his published works by Bible text and by subject.

10. Miscellaneous items. This catalogues material under six headings: A. Biographical Records and Personal Effects; B. Pictures; C. Conduct of Meetings; D. Consideration of B.W. Newton as a writer; E. Items Relating to his Death; F. Reminiscences.

Appendix 1.
    Comparison of the Editions of Thoughts on The Apocalypse.

Appendix 2.
    A Thematic Arrangement of B.W. Newton's Principal Works.

Appendix 3.
    A Select Publications List Relevant to the Controversy of J.N. Darby with B.W. Newton, and his Separation from The Brethren.

www.ingramcontent.com/pod-product-compliance
Lightning Source LLC
Chambersburg PA
CBHW040123130526
44590CB00051B/4408